Econo-Graphics

Incentives
IN INFOGRAPHICS

Christina Hill

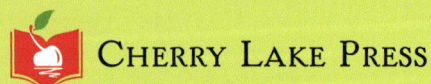

Published in the United States of America by Cherry Lake Publishing Group
Ann Arbor, Michigan
www.cherrylakepublishing.com

Reading Adviser: Beth Walker Gambro, MS, Ed., Reading Consultant, Yorkville, IL

Photo Credits: © Cover, Page 1: ©elena/Getty Images; Page 5: ©Sylfida/Shutterstock, ©iKandy/Shutterstock; Page 7: ©marigis/Shutterstock; Page 8: ©OpenClipart-Vectors/Pixabay; Page 11: ©Artisticco/Shutterstock; Page 12: ©Boy Odachi/Shutterstock; Page 14: ©TAlex/Shutterstock; Page 15: ©Scott Olson/Getty Images; Page 17: ©wera Rodsawang/Getty Images, ©Jeff Mccollough/EyeEm/Getty Images, ©Michael Reinhard/Getty Images, ©Muhammad Owais Khan/Getty Images, ©Maskot/Getty Images, ©Monty Rakusen/Getty Images, ©Andy Sacks/Getty Images; Page 19: ©United States Environmental Protection Agency/Wikimedia, ©Andrew19/Shutterstock, ©Vector Tradition/Shutterstock, ©Irina Strelnikova/Shutterstock; Page 21: ©Faber14/Shutterstock; Page 22: ©Memed_Nurrohmad/Pixabay; Page 23: ©Magura/Shutterstock; Page 25: ©SurfsUp/Shutterstock; Page 26: ©keko-ka/Shutterstock, ©Studio_G/Shutterstock, ©Peter Varga/Shutterstock, ©ideyweb/Shutterstock; Page 27: ©Alvin555/Shutterstock; Page 28: ©OpenClipart-Vectors/Pixabay, ©Sergii Korolko/Shutterstock, © Bens-Photos/Shutterstock; Page 29: ©Benefphic/Shutterstock; Page 30: ©Bonezboyz/Shutterstock

Copyright © 2023 by Cherry Lake Publishing Group

All rights reserved. No part of this book may be reproduced or utilized in any form or by any means without written permission from the publisher.

Cherry Lake Press is an imprint of Cherry Lake Publishing Group.

Library of Congress Cataloging-in-Publication Data
Names: Hill, Christina, author.
Title: Incentives in infographics / Christina Hill.
Description: Ann Arbor, Michigan : Cherry Lake Press, [2023] | Series: Econo-graphics | Includes bibliographical references and index. | Audience: Ages 9-13 | Audience: Grades 4-6 | Summary: "Incentives matter in economics. In this book, readers will learn about tax incentives and rebates that motivate buyers to purchase or invest in certain items. Large-scale and personal real-life examples of incentives are also presented, including facts related to pandemic-era impacts. Colorful and clear graphics, such as maps, charts, and infographics, give readers an alternative to text-heavy sources. Action-based activities will leave students with ideas for how incentives work in economics. This book also includes a glossary, index, suggested reading and websites, and a bibliography"-- Provided by publisher.
Identifiers: LCCN 2022016879 (print) | LCCN 2022016880 (ebook) | ISBN 9781668909997 (hardcover) | ISBN 9781668911594 (paperback) | ISBN 9781668914779 (pdf)
Subjects: LCSH: Tax incentives--Juvenile literature. | Subsidies--Juvenile literature. | Economics--Juvenile literature.
Classification: LCC HJ2336 .H55 2023 (print) | LCC HJ2336 (ebook) | DDC 336.2/06--dc23/eng/20220413
LC record available at https://lccn.loc.gov/2022016879
LC ebook record available at https://lccn.loc.gov/2022016880

Cherry Lake Publishing Group would like to acknowledge the work of the Partnership for 21st Century Learning, a Network of Battelle for Kids. Please visit *http://www.battelleforkids.org/networks/p21* for more information.

Printed in the United States of America

Before embracing a career as an author, **Christina Hill** received a bachelor's degree in English from the University of California, Irvine, and a graduate degree in literature from California State University, Long Beach. When she is not writing about various subjects from sports to economics, Christina can be found hiking, mastering yoga handstands, or curled up with a classic novel. Christina lives in sunny Southern California with her husband, two sons, and beloved dog, Pepper Riley.

CONTENTS

Introduction
What Are Incentives? | 4

Chapter 1
Tax Incentives | 6

Chapter 2
Financial Incentives | 10

Chapter 3
Subsidies | 16

Chapter 4
Negative Incentives | 24

Activity | 30
Learn More | 31
Glossary | 32
Index | 32

INTRODUCTION

What Are Incentives?

In economics, positive and negative **incentives** persuade people to behave in certain ways. **Intrinsic** incentives push people to do something because it makes them feel good. **Extrinsic** incentives push people to do something because of a reward or to avoid punishment. Most economic incentives are extrinsic.

TIMELINE OF CEREAL BOX INCENTIVES

	1909	Kellogg's Corn Flakes offers a mail-order storybook with the purchase of 2 boxes. More than 2.5 million people request the offer.
	1945	Kellogg's adds a pin-backed button to their cereal boxes. It is the first inside-the-box prize.
	1969	Super Sugar Crisps cereal offers a 4-song cut-out record on the back of the box. (It actually plays!)
	1979	Cheerios offers mail-order dartboards.
	1981	Cocoa Puffs offers free bubble gum inside its cereal boxes.
	1990	Jetsons cereal boxes offer a plastic lunar launcher toy.
	2015	Cinnamon Toast Crunch offers droid viewers that include a sneak peek of the latest Star Wars movie.
	2018	Froot Loops offers a chance to win free movie tickets.

CHAPTER 1

Tax Incentives

Tax incentives are benefits issued by a government. If people spend their money on certain things, the government deducts the amount of taxes they owe.

Homeowners are offered a tax incentive called the **mortgage interest** deduction. They can save money on the interest paid on their home **loan**.

Some local governments offer tax breaks to companies who build new offices in their city. This helps provide jobs for people in that area.

Mortgage Interest Deduction

1 A homeowner gets a loan from the bank for $250,000.

2 The interest rate is 4%, and the loan will be paid off in 30 years.

3 At that rate, the homeowner will spend $10,000 the first year in interest alone.

4 The mortgage incentive allows the owner to save $2,500 that year in taxes.

Top 10 U.S. States with Solar Tax Incentives (2021)

Solar energy is more Earth-friendly than fossil fuels such as coal. Solar tax incentives give people extra reasons to "go green."

7. Colorado

6. New Mexico

Some states offer homeowners with solar the choice to deduct 25% of their solar energy expense from their taxes.

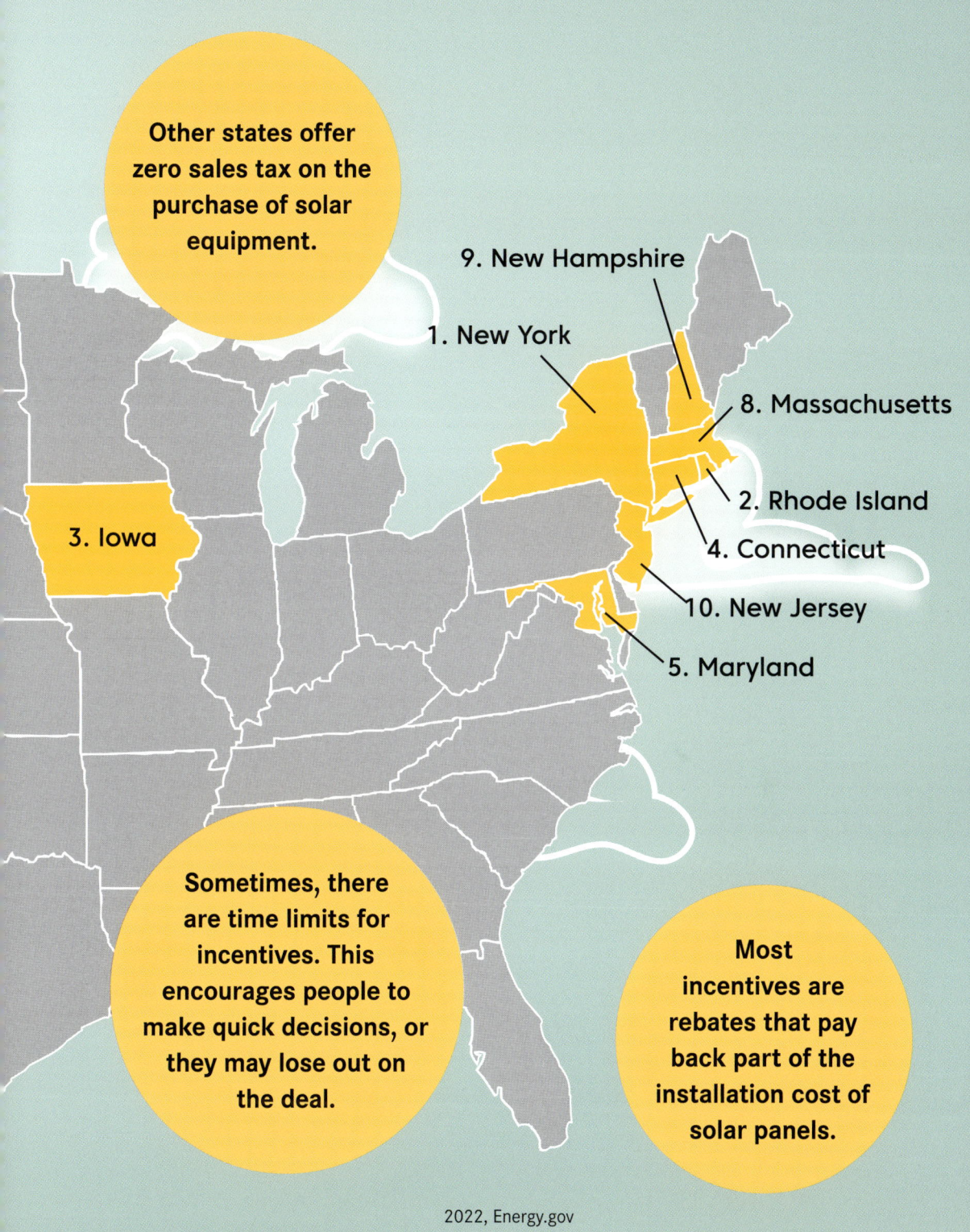

CHAPTER 2

Financial Incentives

Financial incentives are rewards that a company offers. They may be punch cards to earn a free item after several purchases. They might also be "buy one, get one free" offers. Bigger warehouse stores offer memberships, and only members can shop in their stores.

Businesses also offer financial incentives to their employees. They offer raises, bonuses, and even the option to own **stock** in the company to keep employees.

Costco Memberships on the Rise (2014-2020)

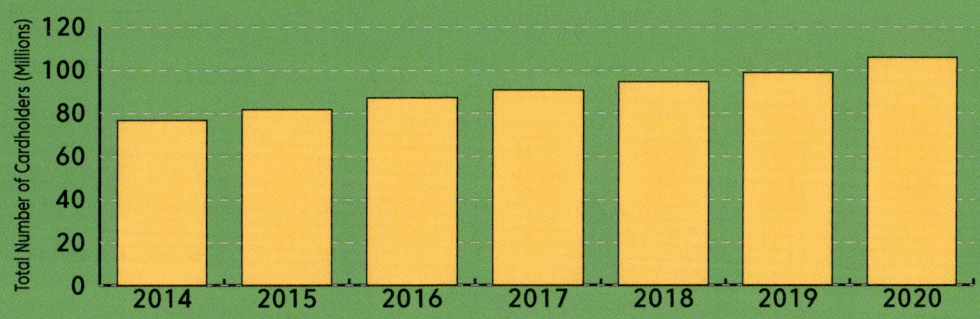

2022, Statista; 2022, Costco

Starbucks and Customer Loyalty

As of March 2021, there were 32,938 Starbucks stores across 80 countries.

Starbucks Rewards Program

- Starbucks has 21.8 million rewards members worldwide.
- Rewards customers contributed 50% of U.S. sales in the first quarter of 2021.

2020, Starbucks Investor News

United Kingdom
1,039

Japan
1,629

South Korea
1,509

China
4,863

2020, Statista; 2020, Starbucks

Get a Shot, Get Fun Stuff!

In 2021, vaccines were created to help fight the COVID-19 pandemic. Many U.S. state governments offered incentives to encourage people to get vaccinated.

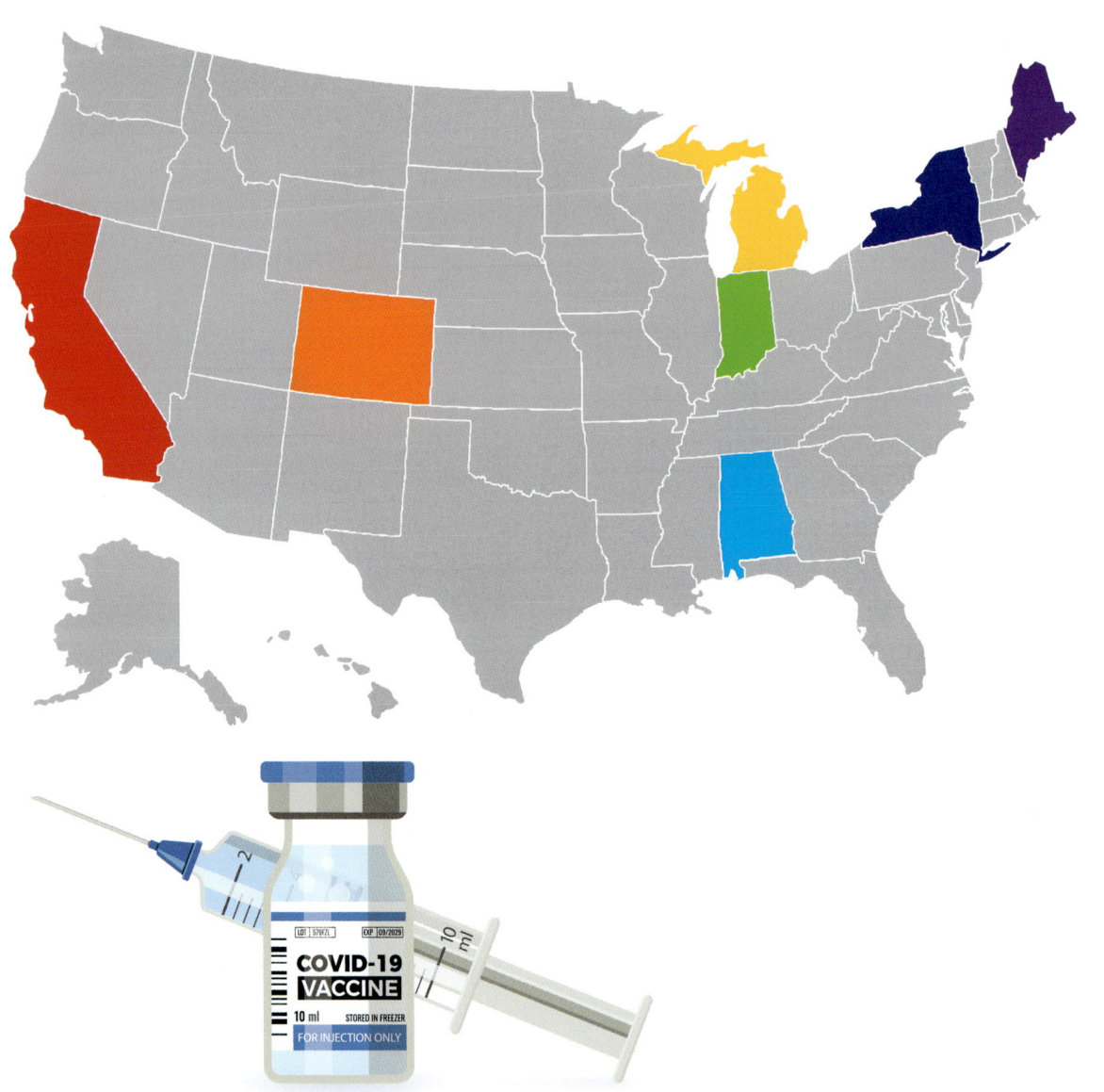

Alabama: The Talladega Superspeedway offered vaccinated people the thrill of driving on the 2.66-mile (4.28-kilometer) track.

California: Some vaccination sites gave away free tickets to any Six Flags Park in California.

Colorado: Vaccinated people could receive $100 Walmart gift cards and $50 Colorado Parks and Wildlife vouchers.

Indiana: Some vaccination sites gave people a box of Girl Scout cookies along with the shot.

Maine: 5,000 day passes to Maine State Parks were given away to vaccinated people.

Michigan: Anyone who brought their friends and neighbors to their COVID-19 vaccine appointments could receive $50 per shot for each appointment.

New York: Kids ages 12 to 17 years old could enter a drawing to win 1 of 50 full-ride scholarships to a New York state college or university.

2021, National Governors Association

Fast Facts

- Krispy Kreme stores across all states offered free donuts to anyone who showed their vaccination card throughout 2021.
- The company gave out more than 2.5 million free donuts!

2021, Krispy Kreme

CHAPTER 3

Subsidies

Subsidies are monies that a government gives to a business to keep prices down or to protect jobs. They are also given to help people in need.

There are two types of subsidies. A direct subsidy provides money to a person or a business, and the government receives nothing in return. **Public assistance** and unemployment benefits are direct subsidies. An indirect subsidy gives a tax break, rebate, or loan from the government to the person or business.

Types of Subsidies

AGRICULTURE

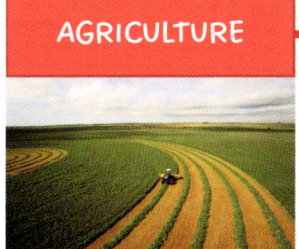

Agriculture subsidies in 2021 made up 23% of total farm earnings.

ELECTRIC CARS

FOSSIL FUEL

U.S. subsidies to the fossil fuel industry are about $20.5 billion per year.

GREEN ENERGY

STEEL

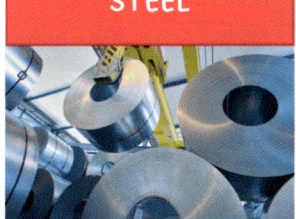

TRANSPORTATION

PUBLIC ASSISTANCE

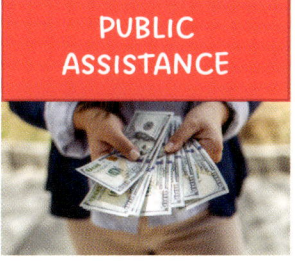

The Department of Transportation offers special grants. In 2021, the grant money funded 90 different transportation improvement projects across 47 states.

2021, EESI; 2021, USDA-ERS; 2022, Department of Transportation

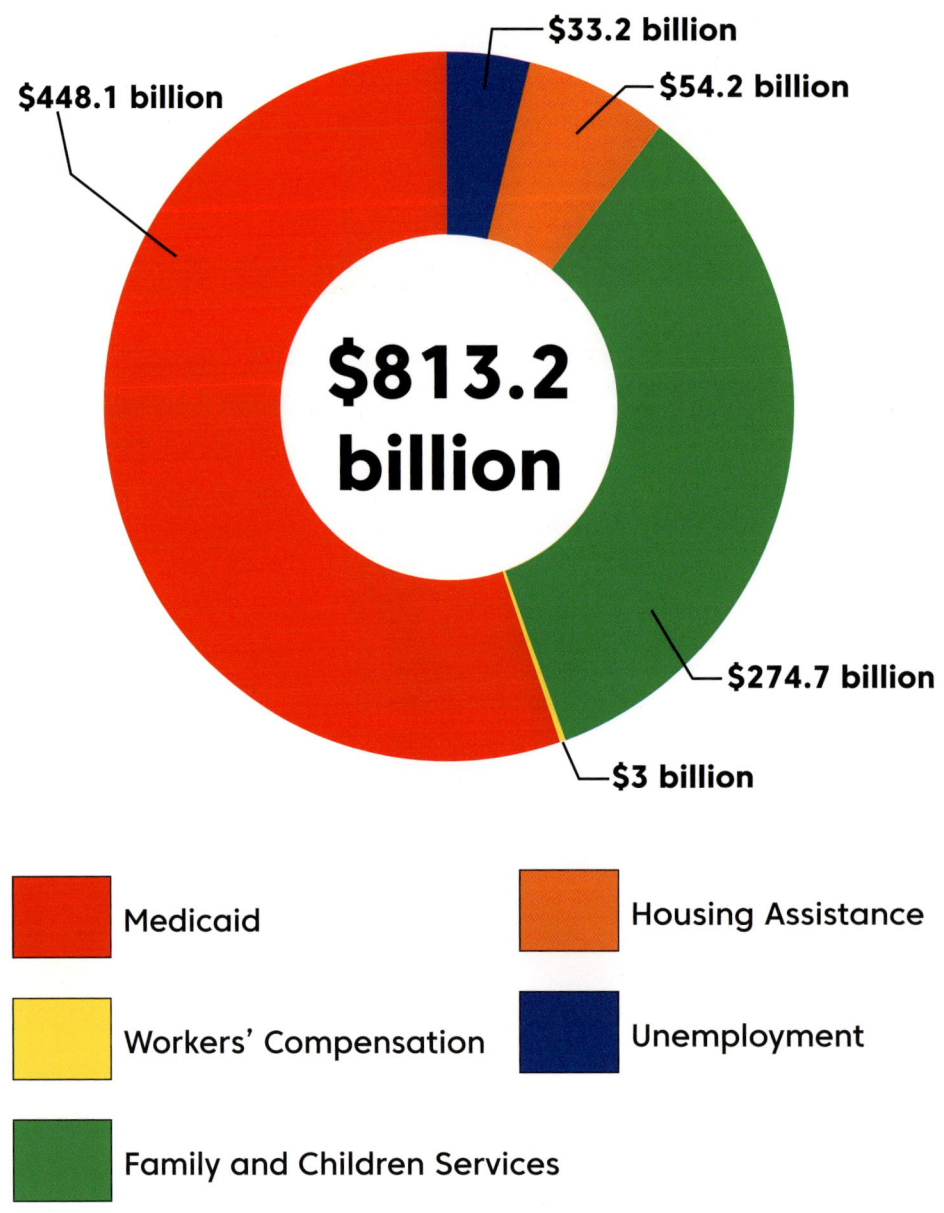

ENERGY STAR Savings

ENERGY STAR partners with the U.S. Environmental Protection Agency (EPA) and the Department of Energy (DOE) to create energy-saving appliances.

Customers can get rebates, or money back, when they purchase ENERGY STAR appliances.

Every dollar the EPA spends on ENERGY STAR results in $350 in savings for businesses and homes.

In 2019, Americans saved $39 billion in energy by using ENERGY STAR appliances.

2020, ENERGY STAR

19

Electric Car Subsidies

- Starting in 2010, the U.S. government offered *consumers* a $7,500 tax credit to buy an electric car.

- In 2010, Tesla received a $465 million loan from the U.S. Department of Energy to make more fuel-efficient vehicles.

- The United Kingdom offers a $3,480 discount for new electric cars.

- In Norway, electric car drivers can get lower taxes and discounts on parking.

2021, World Economic Forum; 2022, Energy.gov

U.S. Agriculture Subsidies in 2020

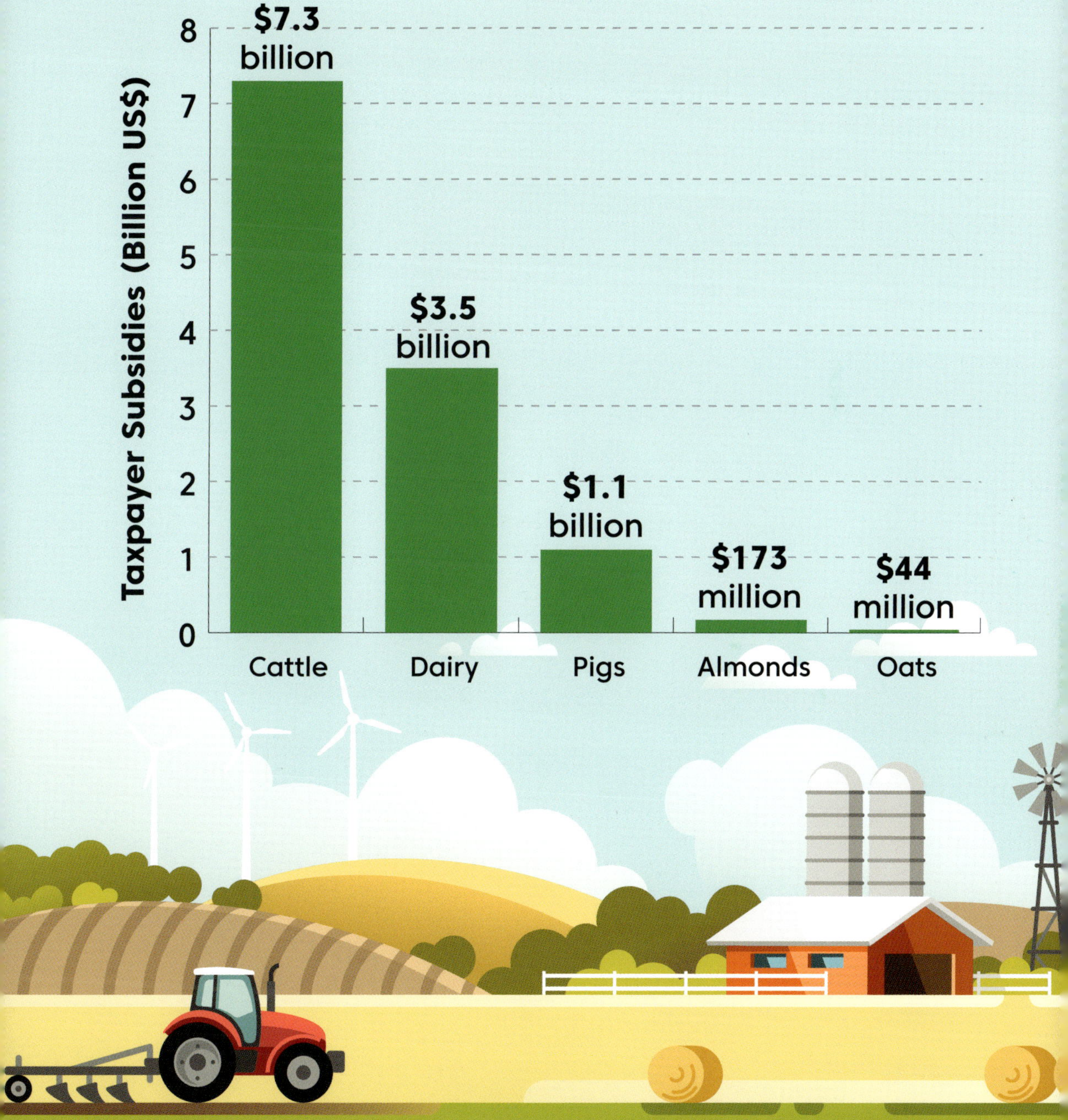

2021, AFA

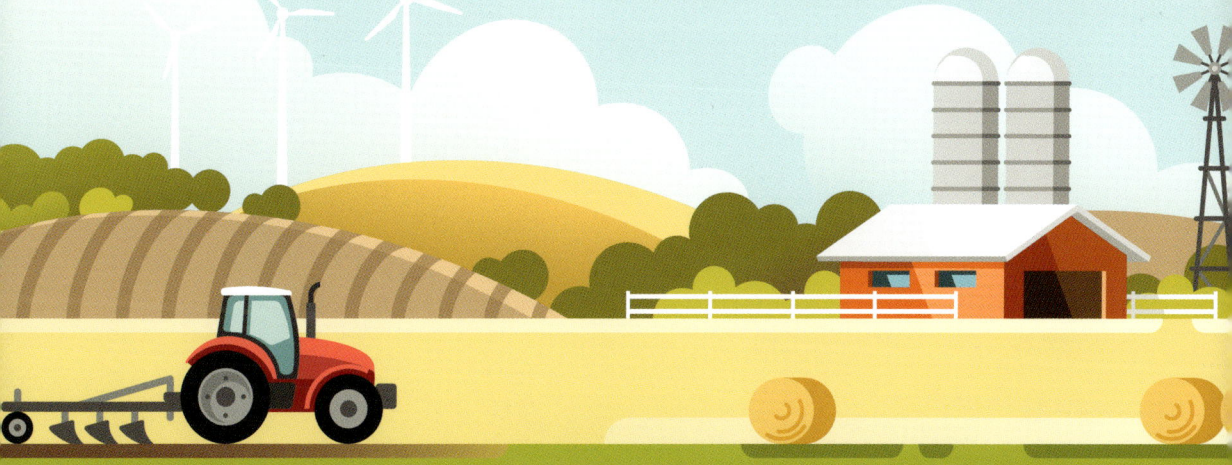

The Cost of College

The U.S. federal government offers subsidized student loans as an incentive for people to go to college. Subsidized loans save students money because the government pays the interest on the loans while students attend school.

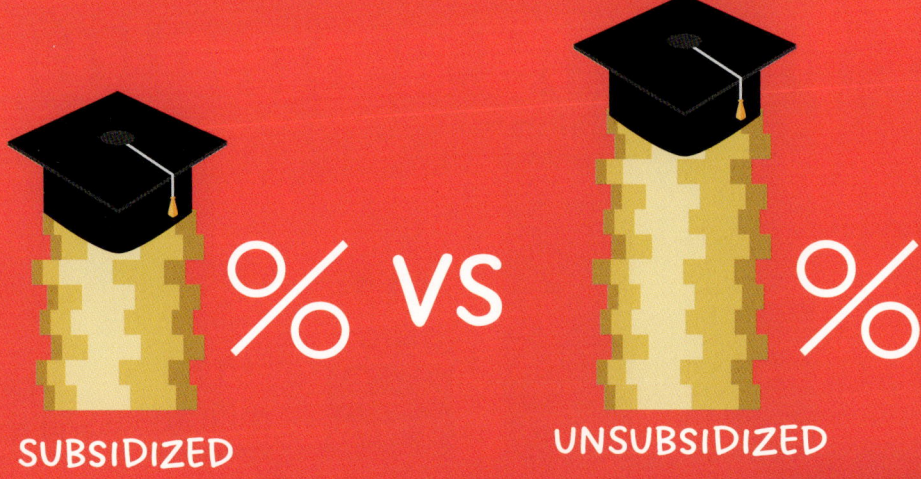

Fast Facts

- The average cost of college in the United States is $35,720 per student per year.
- The average amount owed on a student loan is $39,351.
- Each year, about one-third of all students borrow money to pay for college.
- The average student borrows more than $30,000 to attend school.

2021, Education Data Initiative

How Subsidized Loans Help College Students

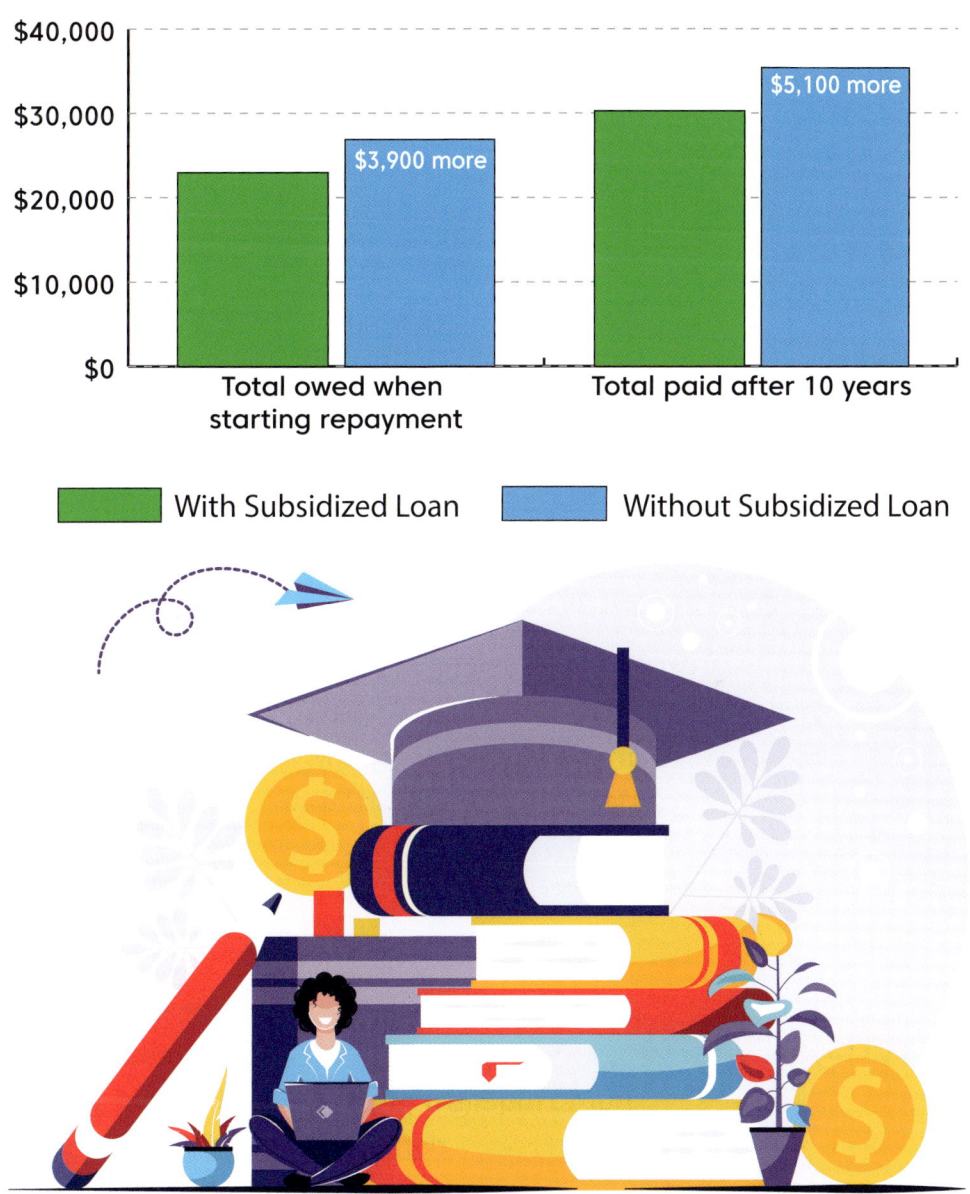

2019, The Institute for College Access & Success

CHAPTER 4

Negative Incentives

Not all incentives are positive ones. Negative incentives are used to shape people's behavior and get them to make better choices. If you are often late to school, you might get detention. If a company creates air pollution, the government might raise its taxes. Drivers who break the law by speeding or refusing to wear a seatbelt will get a ticket. People who litter will be fined.

Workplace Incentives

POSITIVE INCENTIVE
Workers receive a bonus if they make a certain number of parts each week.

NEGATIVE INCENTIVE
Workers do not receive the bonus if they make faulty or broken parts.

Why Countries Choose a Carbon Tax

Climate change is linked to the increased release of greenhouse gases, such as carbon dioxide. Burning coal and other fossil fuels releases carbon dioxide.

Factories cause pollution.

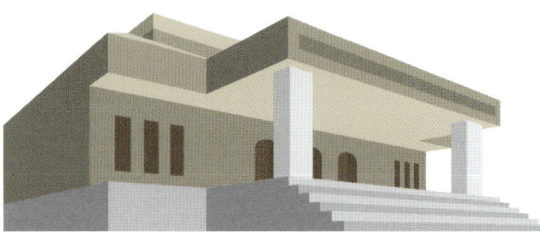

The government issues a carbon tax.

The price of fossil fuels will rise, and consumers will buy less.

Factories and consumers will choose **renewable** energy sources instead.

Pollution levels drop. The environment is healthier.

Top 10 Countries with a Carbon Tax

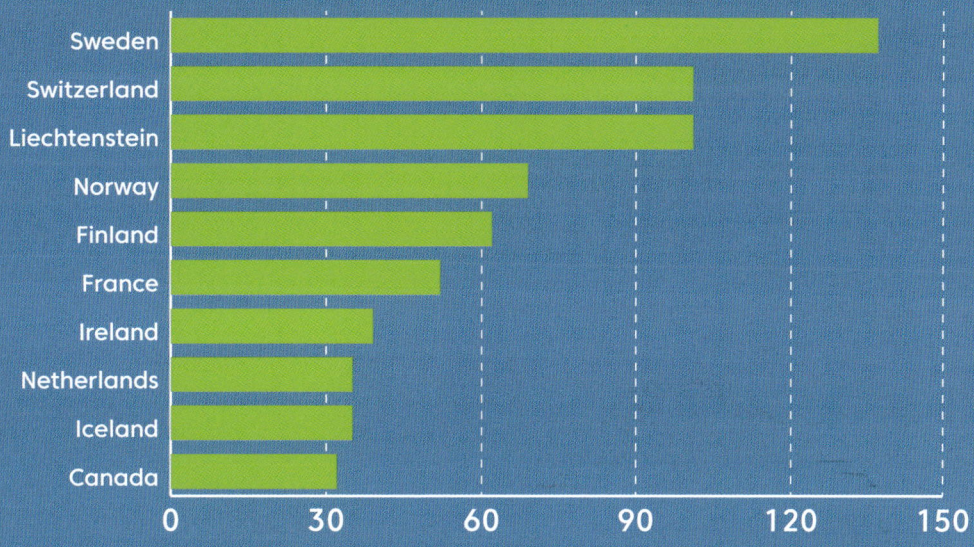

U.S. Dollars per Metric Ton of CO_2

2022, Statista

The Price of Breaking the Law

Each day, 112,000 drivers across the United States receive a speeding ticket for driving over the speed limit.

The average speeding ticket costs $150.

The state with the most speeding tickets in 2021 was Ohio, and 16% of its drivers got one.

Each year, 41 million U.S. drivers receive a speeding ticket.

$6.23 billion is collected each year from speeding tickets.

2021, Insurify; 2021 Hamilton & Associates

Plastic Bans and Fees (2021)

To reduce the use of plastics, some U.S. states have banned single-use plastic bags.

Stores are required to charge a fee (usually 10 cents) to consumers who choose to use a plastic bag.

OF THE 50 U.S. STATES, 26 HAVE PLASTICS BANS IN PLACE.

In San Jose, California, there's been a 76% reduction in creek and river litter since the fee program started. There's also been a 59% drop in park and roadside plastic bag litter and a 69% reduction in plastic bag litter in storm drains.

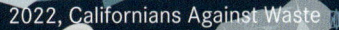
2022, Californians Against Waste

Activity

A Week of Incentives

MENU
- Tacos $2.00
- Chips and Salsa $1.50
- Rice and Beans $2.00
- Soda $1.00
- Churro $1.50

Your older brother is a chef who recently purchased a taco truck. He wants to promote his business and increase sales using incentives.

Help your brother create five financial incentives that will motivate consumers to purchase more food and drinks from his truck. See chapter 2 for ideas.

Create an advertising poster that lists and displays the five incentive options.

Learn More

Books

Dakers, Diane. *Getting Your Money's Worth*. New York, NY: Crabtree Publishing Company, 2017.

Universal Politics. *Why Does the Government Need Our Taxes?* Newark, DE: Speedy Publishing LLC, 2020.

Websites

EconLib: Incentives
https://www.econlib.org/library/Topics/HighSchool/Incentives.html

PBS Learning Media: Wetlands: The Drain Game
https://tpt.pbslearningmedia.org/resource/4aeab145-9964-47d0-a0db-7434cb01ddbc/wetlands-the-drain-game-policies-and-incentives/?student=true

Bibliography

Boysen, Ole, Kirsten Boysen-Urban, Harvey Bradford, and Jean Balié. "Could Higher Junk Food Taxes Reduce Obesity?" February 2020. https://www.sciencejournalforkids.org/wp-content/uploads/2020/02/tax_article.pdf

White, David. "Subsidy: Grant for the Greater Good." Social Studies for Kids. Accessed February 4, 2022. https://socialstudiesforkids.com/articles/economics/subsidy.htm

Glossary

climate change (KLY-mit chaynj) the shifts in Earth's temperatures and weather patterns over time

consumers (kuhn-SOO-murz) people who buy goods and services

extrinsic (ik-STRIN-sik) coming from the outside of something

financial (fy-NAN-shuhl) relating to money

incentives (in-SEN-tivz) things that push a person to do something or work harder

interest (IN-tur-ist) the money paid by a borrower for the use of borrowed money

intrinsic (in-TRIN-sik) coming from within; a natural part of something

loan (LOHN) an amount of money that is given to someone with a promise that it will be paid back

mortgage (MOHR-gij) a legal agreement created when a person borrows money to buy a house

public assistance (PUHB-lik uh-SIS-tuhns) a government program that helps poor or unemployed people pay for their needs

renewable (rih-NOO-uh-buhl) able to be restored or replaced

stock (STAHK) a share of the value of a company that can be bought, sold, or traded as an investment

tax (TAKS) an amount of money that a government requires citizens to pay that is used to fund the things the government provides for them

Index

agriculture, 17, 21
COVID-19 pandemic, 14, 15
electric cars, 17, 20
ENERGY STAR, 19
home loans, 6, 7
incentives
   cereal box, 5
   financial, 10, 30
   negative, 4, 24, 25, 26, 27
   solar, 8, 9
   tax, 6, 7, 8, 9, 26, 27
   vaccine, 14, 15

Krispy Kreme, 15
memberships, 10, 11
public assistance, 16, 17, 18
rewards, 4, 10, 13
Starbucks, 12, 13
student loans, 22, 23
subsidies, 16, 17, 20, 21, 22, 23
tax breaks, 6, 16